DARING & Disruptive playbook

Think
BIG
beyond
yourself,
break out
of the
BOX.

Any views and opinions expressed herein are strictly the author's own and do not represent those of The Messenger Group.

A CIP catalogue of this book is available from the National Library of Australia.

Messenger, Lisa
Daring & Disruptive Playbook
ISBN 978-0-646-93087-9

First published in 2014 by The Messenger Group Pty Ltd
PO Box H241
Australia Square NSW 1215

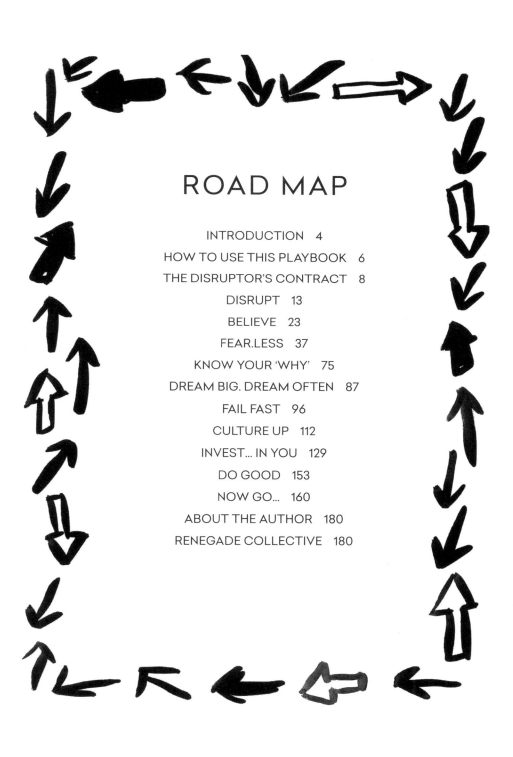

ROAD MAP

INTRODUCTION

I always try to listen and react fast to feedback. How else can you grow authentically as an entrepreneur and as a brand, if you're not taking on board the opinion of the people who really matter? So when a number of friends and fans of *Daring & Disruptive* told me they loved it (phew!), but that they'd also love a workbook where they could put their bubbling thoughts, dreams, ideas and my advice into practice – I jumped into action.

My mind was made up when, at a recent event held by *The Collective*, a reader pulled a copy of *Daring & Disruptive* from her handbag to show me. Every page was covered in doodled graffiti – she'd written her ideas down the margins and highlighted quotes in fluorescent marker pen. It was a chaotic, colourful, total mess. It was amazing! I loved how inspired she was and that I'd played a role in it. What a gift.

But her scribbles were overflowing the page. What she needed was more space, lots of blank pages nearby, perhaps even some prompts to continue her subconscious flow... what she needed was a workbook. In fact, the idea had already crossed my mind, during one of my midnight blanket-wrestling brainstorming sessions (you know the ones?).

I wrote *Daring & Disruptive* as a companion for entrepreneurs and forward-thinkers with sage advice and some thoughts to kick them into action, because so many people asked how I did it ('it' being the launch of a successful magazine into a struggling market when I had absolutely no media experience). I wanted to show that anything is possible. Absolutely anything.

I'm not an expert or guru, but I hope the pages in this book will be a starting point. It also won't have all the answers but will help you find some. But, I know the hardest part of being an entrepreneur can be the first daunting step. So allow me to point you in the right direction. This playbook isn't a business plan in the conventional sense (when am I ever conventional?). It's not a practical template to develop a product, find a supplier or organise your finances.

This book, full of prompts, is a journey of self-exploration for anyone who has a spark of an idea, an entrepreneurial itch or just a sense they're destined to make a difference in the world. That's not an arrogant thought – we all have the potential within us.

I hope this book helps you to identify your purpose, shape your idea & make your dreams a reality.

xx Lisa

HOW TO USE
THIS PLAYBOOK

I have written journals and diaries in some form or another since I was a free-spirited schoolgirl. My head was always so full of ideas that I soon realised there wasn't space for them all, so I started putting pen to paper – whether it was the places I dreamed of travelling, the hobbies I dreamed of mastering or how I planned to change the world (or at least one corner of it at a time).

The best thing about writing your thoughts down is, not only can it help you identify your values, passions and purpose, but it also gives you a permanent reminder – a 'thought timeline'. The questions in this playbook aren't just designed to be answered once – you can revisit, re-assess and see how your mindset shifts over days, weeks, months and years!

It also helps to put your priorities into perspective. Remember when as a 13-year-old, you wrote in your diary that you would just *die* if your crush didn't notice you? The real-world problem seemed so catastrophic at the time, but (hopefully) now you are laughing at the memory.

In the same way, I want this playbook to be a place for you to process your dreams, express your fears and prepare to take the leap (whatever you decide that leap needs to be). There are questions, exercises and a whole heap of scrapbook pages to stick in whatever is inspiring you, whether it's quotes you've read, interviews from magazines or visuals of how you'd like your career, your life, your workspace or your world to look.

Feel free to skip over questions that don't excite you – scribble over them, rip out pages, get rebellious, graffiti a moustache on my photo! I give you full permission. This book is for you to use exactly as you wish. Write, stick, doodle, sketch. I won't be offended if you don't colour between the lines. In fact, I'll be impressed.

Now... go!

WHAT you will need:

- 📖 This playbook ☑
- Something to write with ☑ ✏️
- A sense of ·wonder· ☑

THE DISRUPTOR'S CONTRACT

I, ——————————,

commit to being
daring + disruptive ...

I promise to allow this playbook to be a place where I let my mind wander, my dreams fly and my expectations soar. I solemnly swear to banish the words 'should' and 'wish'. I will allow myself to break out of the box and embrace my crazy uniqueness.

I promise my inner entrepreneur that, no matter what ideas erupt on these pages, I will not belittle them or dismiss them without exploring them first. I vow to write as a rebel, a rule breaker and a game changer until this playbook is filled – and hopefully throughout my life from this point on.

Signature:
Date:

↖ sign here

Today
you
will
trust
yourself.

embrace
the good,
the bad
& the
wonderful
that makes
you, you.

Channel the energy of a child & create as much mischief as you can.

DISRUPT

REMEMBER A TIME THAT YOU REBELLED

AS A CHILD:

AS A TEENAGER:

AS AN ADULT:

WHO DO YOU ADMIRE FOR THEIR DARING ATTITUDE, AND WHY?

IN YOUR FAMILY:

IN YOUR FRIENDSHIP CIRCLE:

AT WORK OR IN BUSINESS:

IN LIFE GENERALLY:

Daring

adjective:
to bravely go
where others
won't.

Disruptive

adjective :
to shake things
up & make your
mark on
the world .

MIND THE GAP

IF YOU COULD SHAKE UP ONE INDUSTRY WHAT WOULD
IT BE?

HOW WOULD YOU TURN IT ON ITS HEAD?

WHAT BUSINESS OR NEW START-UP DO YOU MOST ADMIRE?

HOW ARE THEY DOING THINGS DIFFERENTLY?

IF YOU WORK WITHIN A CORPORATE, HOW COULD YOU DISRUPT THE STATUS QUO?

HOW COULD YOU TURN YOUR TEAM, YOUR DEPARTMENT OR THE ENTIRE THING ON ITS HEAD?

WHAT OTHER STAFF – OR INTERNAL DISRUPTORS –
DO YOU ADMIRE?

HOW ARE THEY DOING THINGS DIFFERENTLY?

my notes...

BELIEVE

ME: THE ENTREPRENEUR

In the first chapter of *Daring & Disruptive* I talk about the importance of unwavering, insatiable self-belief, trusting your gut and playing to your strengths. Because if you don't understand yourself – your motives, your goals, your dreams – then how on earth will anyone else? The following questions might feel like a corporate job interview (sorry for the C-word) but they're the building blocks for the beginning of your (ad)venture.

HOBBIES AND INTERESTS:

WHAT I'M GREAT AT:

WHAT I'M TERRIBLE AT:

WHAT I'M PASSIONATE ABOUT:

WHO I ADMIRE:

WHAT I VALUE:

☐ friends
☒ family
☐ solitude

WHAT I AM CURRENTLY KNOWN FOR:

MY HIDDEN TALENTS:

HOW MY BEST FRIENDS WOULD DESCRIBE ME:

HOW MY LAST BOSS WOULD DESCRIBE ME:

HOW MY COLLEAGUES WOULD DESCRIBE ME:

☐ creative
☐ detailed
☐ outgoing

THE BEST WORKDAY OF MY LIFE:

Wake up at...
Spend my morning...
End the day feeling...

THE WORST WORKDAY OF MY LIFE:

MY IDEAL DAY:

ACHIEVEMENTS I LOOK BACK ON WITH PRIDE:

PITCHES, PROJECTS OR WORK ACTIVITIES I HAVE
COMPLETELY NAILED:

GREAT THINGS OTHERS
HAVE SAID ABOUT ME:

GREAT THINGS OTHERS HAVE SAID ABOUT MY WORK:

ME: THE WORLD CHANGER

WHICH WORDS BEST DESCRIBE YOU NOW:

imaginative   dynamic

focused genuine   dependabl

motivated   trustnorthy   genero

authentic

WHICH WORDS BEST DESCRIBE WHO YOU WANT TO BE:

objective   hard-working

courageous   sincere

                        ambitious

rule breaking

                    responsible

        loyal

                    adventurous

sympathetic   tenacious

You can't bottle fear, but it doesn't have to drown you.

FEAR.LESS

WE'VE ALL FELT FEARFUL.
REMEMBER IT ISN'T FATAL.

THE FIRST TIME I SWAM IN THE OCEAN I FELT...

ON MY FIRST DATE I FELT...

ON MY FIRST DAY IN MY CURRENT JOB I FELT...

THE FIRST TIME I HAD TO MAKE A BUSINESS PITCH I FELT...

(If you hadn't overcome those fears, think of everything you'd have missed out on.)

SLEEPLESS NIGHTS – AND HOW TO OVERCOME THEM.

For me, things are a hundred times worse at night – your mind races and whatever you are facing suddenly feels insurmountable. If you're like me – or perhaps fear strikes you by day – keep this playbook by your bed or in your bag so the next time you wake up in the middle of the night paralysed by 'what ifs' or feel the paralysis striking by day, you can grab a pen and put your worries into perspective one by one.

WORRY #1
WHAT ARE YOU WORRYING ABOUT?

WILL IT MATTER 10 MINUTES FROM NOW?

WILL IT MATTER 10 MONTHS FROM NOW?

WILL IT MATTER 10 YEARS FROM NOW?

WILL IT MATTER 10 DECADES FROM NOW?

WHAT'S THE WORST-CASE SCENARIO?

WHO COULD HELP YOU SOLVE THE PROBLEM OR EXPLORE
WAYS TO CHANGE IT?

AND TO REVISIT LATER: DID THE ISSUE/SITUATION YOU
FEARED EVER MATERIALISE?

HOW DID YOU DEAL WITH IT AND WAS IT AS BAD AS
YOU EXPECTED?

(Don't miss the sun
today worrying about
the rain tomorrow.)

WORRY #2
WHAT ARE YOU WORRYING ABOUT?

WILL IT MATTER 10 MINUTES FROM NOW?

WILL IT MATTER 10 MONTHS FROM NOW?

WILL IT MATTER 10 YEARS FROM NOW?

WILL IT MATTER 10 DECADES FROM NOW?

WHAT'S THE WORST-CASE SCENARIO?

WHO COULD HELP YOU SOLVE THE PROBLEM OR EXPLORE
WAYS TO CHANGE IT?

AND TO REVISIT LATER: DID THE ISSUE/SITUATION YOU
FEARED EVER MATERIALISE?

HOW DID YOU DEAL WITH IT AND WAS IT AS BAD AS
YOU EXPECTED?

(sometimes you just
need to take a
deep breath.)

share
&
scare
alike.

The journey of business generally has given me its fair share of difficult moments, but The Collective itself has given me the most sleepless nights (believe me!).

If fear is an issue for you, read my tips on going from worrier to warrior in Daring + Disruptive (P.55)

WORRY #3
WHAT ARE YOU WORRYING ABOUT?

WILL IT MATTER 10 MINUTES FROM NOW?

WILL IT MATTER 10 MONTHS FROM NOW?

WILL IT MATTER 10 YEARS FROM NOW?

WILL IT MATTER 10 DECADES FROM NOW?

WHAT'S THE WORST-CASE SCENARIO?

WHO COULD HELP YOU SOLVE THE PROBLEM OR EXPLORE
WAYS TO CHANGE IT?

AND TO REVISIT LATER: DID THE ISSUE/SITUATION YOU
FEARED EVER MATERIALISE?

HOW DID YOU DEAL WITH IT AND WAS IT AS BAD AS
YOU EXPECTED?

WORRY #4
WHAT ARE YOU WORRYING ABOUT?

WILL IT MATTER 10 MINUTES FROM NOW?

WILL IT MATTER 10 MONTHS FROM NOW?

WILL IT MATTER 10 YEARS FROM NOW?

WILL IT MATTER 10 DECADES FROM NOW?

WHAT'S THE WORST-CASE SCENARIO?

WHO COULD HELP YOU SOLVE THE PROBLEM OR EXPLORE
WAYS TO CHANGE IT?

AND TO REVISIT LATER: DID THE ISSUE/SITUATION YOU
FEARED EVER MATERIALISE?

HOW DID YOU DEAL WITH IT AND WAS IT AS BAD AS
YOU EXPECTED?

THE SHY ONE'S GUIDE TO PUBLIC SPEAKING

Is public speaking a problem for you? As I admit in *Daring & Disruptive* (page 47) I was once petrified of public speaking and it is well documented as one of the top five fears in the world. These days, you need to wrestle the microphone away from me to stop me talking. So how did I overcome my fears? I took some time out to unpack them, understand them and look for ways to ease them. Then I had to do one important thing: face them. Give it a go for yourself.

THE PROBLEM

I feel uncomfortable speaking in front of a crowd because:

☐ I WORRY I'LL FORGET MY WORDS

☐ I THINK OTHERS ARE FUNNIER, MORE CHARISMATIC OR MORE KNOWLEDGEABLE

☐ WHAT IF SOMEONE ASKS A QUESTION I CAN'T ANSWER?

☐ WHAT IF NOBODY CAN HEAR ME?

☐ I NEVER KNOW WHAT TO WEAR

☐ I NEVER KNOW HOW TO STAND

☐ I MIGHT SEEM BORING

☐ I WON'T SEE ANY FAMILIAR FACES

☐ I WILL SEE TOO MANY FAMILIAR FACES

☐ IT REMINDS ME OF BEING AT SCHOOL

Cut out and keep me!

SOME SOLUTIONS

#1 WEAR SOMETHING AMAZING

Find an outfit that makes you feel most confident and authentic. Perhaps it's not even in your wardrobe yet. When you imagine the coolest, most confident version of you, what are you wearing?

#2 BOOST YOUR KNOWLEDGE

Ask yourself, how can I boost my knowledge of the subject? What could I read beforehand? Is there a TED talk I can watch, white papers I can soak up or a book I can read to prepare?

#3 LEARN FROM THE BEST

Which public speakers do you admire and have they ever given tips on public speaking? Read about their tips or watch YouTube clips of their presentations.

#4 TRY IT FOR YOURSELF, BY YOURSELF

Now, practise in front of the mirror (I know, you're probably squirming) and ask yourself: How do I feel and look most comfortable – standing, sitting or a combo?

#5 FACE THE FEAR OUT LOUD

Finally, write the introduction to a speech where you're honest and admit that you're nervous. Read this aloud. You might find that just confessing your apprehension helps you feel more authentic and loosens your tongue.

Dreams → Plans

If I hired people just like me, we would end up with an insanely visionary workplace with all the ideas in the world but no one detail-orientated enough to turn those dreams into plans!

IDENTIFY YOUR WEAKNESS – AND WHO CAN HELP YOU

Let's be honest, absolutely no one is the whole package – and if they claim to be, they're kidding themselves. As I explain in my book, a key to combating fear is to have a solid team in place for turbulent times to help you walk through them. When it comes to recruiting, my approach is to hire my weaknesses (*Daring & Disruptive*, page 112). It's time to identify yours and then fill in the knowledge gaps.

WEAKNESS 1:
IS THERE AN EXPERT IN MY EXISTING NETWORK WHO CAN HELP ME WITH IT?

IF NOT, WHERE COULD I FIND SOMEONE WHO CAN?

WEAKNESS 2:
IS THERE AN EXPERT IN MY EXISTING NETWORK WHO CAN
HELP ME WITH IT?

IF NOT, WHERE COULD I FIND SOMEONE WHO CAN?

WEAKNESS 3:
IS THERE AN EXPERT IN MY EXISTING NETWORK WHO CAN
HELP ME WITH IT?

IF NOT, WHERE COULD I FIND SOMEONE WHO CAN?

WEAKNESS 4:
IS THERE AN EXPERT IN MY EXISTING NETWORK WHO CAN
HELP ME WITH IT?

IF NOT, WHERE COULD I FIND SOMEONE WHO CAN?

I'm crazy, frenetic...

I think a million miles an hour.
Closed minds don't pass go.

BUILD YOUR SELF-BELIEF BANK

Why do the criticisms we receive get more internal airtime than our compliments or a celebration of our achievements? They don't have to. To balance it out, don't let compliments slip your mind – write them within these pages.

POSITIVE FEEDBACK I HAVE RECEIVED FROM BUSINESS MEETINGS:

COMPLIMENTARY COMMENTS FROM PEOPLE ON SOCIAL MEDIA:

SUPPORTIVE TEXTS AND EMAILS FROM FRIENDS OR COLLEAGUES:

TOUGH SITUATIONS I HAVE HANDLED WELL:

THANK YOU NOTES OR MESSAGES RECEIVED FROM
CUSTOMERS OR COLLEAGUES:

* In Daring + Disruptive (P.33)
I share some of my small
moments of validation,
which might be helpful
prompts for you too.

STOP THE SELF-SABOTAGE

Are you your own worst enemy? We can all be prone to a little self-sabotage, so take a few moments to examine if you have patterns of this often subtle, but debilitating behaviour.

I HELD MYSELF BACK IN MY CAREER WHEN:

I HELD MYSELF BACK IN MY LOVE LIFE WHEN:

I HELD MYSELF BACK IN MY FAMILY WHEN:

I HELD MYSELF BACK IN FRIENDSHIPS WHEN:

Be on your own side

"Those who say life is knocking them down and giving them a tough time are usually the first to beat themselves up. Be on your own side."

— Rasheed Ogunlaru

I HELD MYSELF BACK IN MY HEALTH AND FITNESS
GOALS WHEN:

I HELD MYSELF BACK FINANCIALLY WHEN:

I WILL PROPEL MYSELF FORWARD IN MY CAREER BY:

If you are holding yourself back,
then you also have the power
to propel yourself forward...

I WILL PROPEL MYSELF FORWARD IN MY LOVE LIFE BY:

I WILL PROPEL MYSELF FORWARD IN MY FAMILY BY:

I WILL PROPEL MYSELF FORWARD IN FRIENDSHIPS BY:

I WILL PROPEL MYSELF FORWARD IN HEALTH AND FITNESS BY:

I WILL PROPEL MYSELF FORWARD FINANCIALLY BY:

$

$

$

$

$

$

$

$

$

$

$

express change adore
wonder disrupt rest
celebrate giv
dream think
chase smile
laugh discover breathe
rebel search explore
play transform inspire
innovate observ
activate challenge
move empower energise
wander dare
experiment love admir

express change adore
wonder disrupt rest
celebrate give
dream smile think
chase
laugh discover breathe
rebel search explore
lay transform inspire
innovate observe
activate challenge
move empower energise
wander dare
experiment love admire

your mantra scrapbook

Stick your favourite quotes here, for a poignant reminder when your fears start to take hold, tomorrow can *always* be better.

Dust settles, people shouldn't!

fail fast...
fail often

my scrapbook ...

It's
cool
to be
KIND

Never hope
for more
than you
work for.

My goal
in life
is simple:
I want to
live every day
as full
as possible.

KNOW YOUR
'WHY'

WHY DO YOU WANT TO BE DARING AND DISRUPTIVE?

- [ ] FUN
- [ ] FAME
- [ ] FORTUNE
- [ ] EXCITEMENT
- [ ] MAKE MONEY
- [ ] MAKE A DIFFERENCE
- [ ] SHARE A MESSAGE
- [ ] SOLVE A PROBLEM
- [ ] PROMOTE A CAUSE
- [ ] INSPIRE OTHERS
- [ ] LEAVE A LEGACY
- [ ] FILL A GAP IN THE MARKET
- [ ] CREATE SOMETHING NEW
- [ ] MY FRIENDS/FAMILY KEEP TELLING ME TO
- [ ] OTHER:

WHY DO YOU WANT TO TAKE THE STEP NOW?

☐ I HAVE THE TIME

☐ I HAVE THE MONEY

☐ IT FEELS RIGHT

☐ THE MARKET IS READY

☐ I'VE RUN OUT OF EXCUSES

☐ IT'S NOW OR NEVER

☐ IT'S KEEPING ME AWAKE AT NIGHT

☐ I FEEL SUDDENLY INSPIRED

☐ I DON'T HAVE RESPONSIBILITIES HOLDING ME BACK

☐ OTHER:

WHAT ARE YOU PASSIONATE ABOUT RIGHT NOW?

- ☐ FOOD
- ☐ TRAVEL
- ☐ FASHION
- ☐ BEAUTY
- ☐ TECHNOLOGY
- ☐ INNOVATION
- ☐ EDUCATION
- ☐ MUSIC
- ☐ SOCIAL CAUSES
- ☐ CONNECTING PEOPLE
- ☐ CULTURE/PEOPLE GROUPS
- ☐ TV/FILM/ENTERTAINMENT
- ☐ ENVIRONMENTAL ISSUES
- ☐ OTHER:

THE MOMENT OF TRUTH

WHAT IS THE LAST THING YOU THINK ABOUT BEFORE
YOU FALL ASLEEP?

WHAT IS THE FIRST THING YOU THINK ABOUT WHEN
YOU WAKE UP?

ARE YOU THE SAME PERSON AT WORK AND AT HOME? IF NOT,
WHAT IS THE DIFFERENCE BETWEEN THE TWO?

HOW WOULD YOU DESCRIBE THE MOST AUTHENTIC
VERSION OF YOURSELF?

HOW DO YOU WANT TO BE REMEMBERED?

(I will leave this world
better than I found it.)

ASK THE OUTSIDE WORLD

PEOPLE OFTEN SEE THINGS IN US THAT WE HAVEN'T RECOGNISED OURSELVES. WHEN FRIENDS COME TO YOU FOR ADVICE OR HELP, WHAT IS IT USUALLY ABOUT?

DO YOU HAVE A HOBBY THAT PEOPLE CONTINUALLY COMPLIMENT YOU ON?

DO YOU HAVE A CREATIVE OUTLET YOU'VE DONE SINCE YOU
WERE A CHILD?

HAVE YOU TAKEN UP A NEW HOBBY OR PASSION AS
AN ADULT?

A string
of small
failures
can push
you on with
knowledge
& wisdom.

The BIG question

IF MONEY WAS NO OBJECT, HOW WOULD YOU LOVE
TO SPEND EVERY DAY?

Forget the off switch!

keep the ideas flowing.
In times of crazy, unfocused
buzzing, some of the
best ideas are formed.

DREAM BIG.
DREAM OFTEN.

IDEAS ARE ALL AROUND US

Daring and disruptive entrepreneurs never switch off. You never know what everyday object, overheard conversation or shopping receipt you find in the bottom of a supermarket trolley that will trigger inspiration.

Spend time teaching yourself how to daydream with your eyes open (yes, it's a trick I've learned over the years). Work through the scenarios adjacent and write down everything you see – I mean everything – in great detail.

IN YOUR BEDROOM:

IN A CAFÉ:

IN A TRAFFIC JAM (WHEN YOU'RE NOT DRIVING):

AT THE PARK OR BEACH:

WHILE YOU'RE EXERCISING:

WHILE YOU'RE RESTING OR MEDITATING:

IN YOUR OFFICE:

AT THE HOME OF FRIENDS/FAMILY:

HOW WOULD YOUR PRODUCT OR SERVICE IMPROVE SOMEONE'S LIFE? WHAT'S THE PAIN POINT YOU ARE SERVICING?

- [ ] MAKE IT MORE CONVENIENT

- [ ] HELP THEM SAVE/MAKE MONEY

- [ ] MAKE PEOPLE HAPPIER

- [ ] MAKE PEOPLE HEALTHIER

- [ ] HELP THEM CONNECT WITH OTHERS

- [ ] MAKE A COMPLEX TASK SIMPLER

- [ ] IMPROVE GENERAL WELLBEING

- [ ] EDUCATE AND INFORM

- [ ] ENTERTAIN AND FASCINATE

- [ ] OTHER:

IF MONEY WAS NO OBJECT, WHAT PROBLEM WOULD YOU LIKE TO SOLVE?

IN YOUR OWN LIFE:

IN YOUR BEST FRIEND'S LIFE:

IN YOUR PARENT'S LIFE:

IN YOUR LOCAL COMMUNITY:

IN YOUR COUNTRY OR ACROSS THE WORLD:

CHOOSE ONE OF THE ABOVE AND ASK YOURSELF:
HOW COULD YOU SCALE THIS BACK TO YOUR BUDGET?

There are two
types of
people
out there
— the 'implementers'
and the
'gunnas'.

Don't be
a gunna!

FAIL FAST

FROM PASSION TO PROJECT

Once I have an idea, I write down everything I can possibly muster up – it's a word vomit (pardon the visual) that covers everything in no particular order.

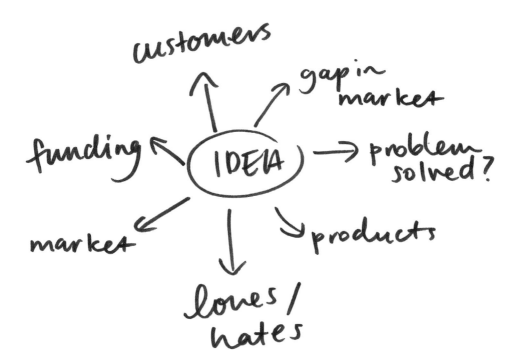

word Map Your vision

IDEA #1
MY IDEA AND THE WORDS THAT FORM IT:

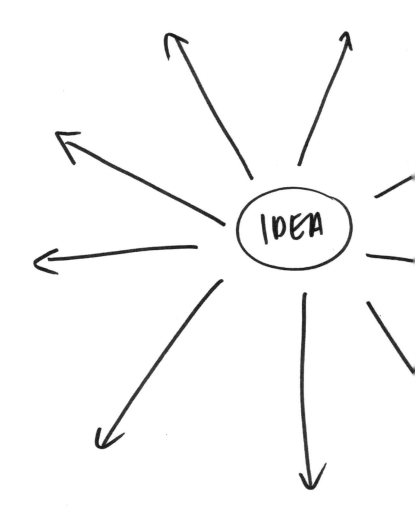

IDEA #2
MY IDEA AND THE WORDS THAT FORM IT:

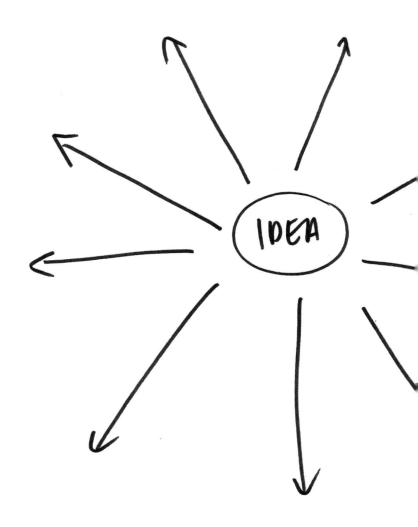

IDEA #3
MY IDEA AND THE WORDS THAT FORM IT:

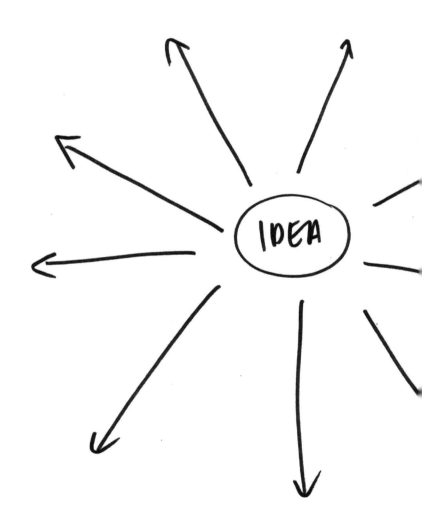

THE MARKET

Pick your favourite idea and brainstorm it further. Ask yourself: who is my target audience? Think about their:

✗ AGE

✗ GENDER

✗ CAREER/OCCUPATION

✗ INCOME

✗ LOCATION

✗ FAMILY (MARRIED, CHILDREN)

✗ EDUCATION

✗ LIFE ASPIRATIONS

✗ INTERESTS

✗ ROLE MODELS

GOOD, BAD OR JUST THE WRONG TIME?

I don't really believe in lengthy business plans, as you'll read in *Daring & Disruptive* (page 88). Instead, before I invest in an idea I do quick-fire market research. It's amazing how much feedback you can get within a week of a light-bulb moment.

Crowd-research your network; poll friends and family, choose a social media platform and post your idea or send an email to a potential partner. Do they bite?

Now go and do some quick Market research...

NAME:

CONTACT DETAILS:

RELATIONSHIP TO YOU:

COMMENTS/FEEDBACK:

NAME:

CONTACT DETAILS:

RELATIONSHIP TO YOU:

COMMENTS/FEEDBACK:

NAME:

CONTACT DETAILS:

RELATIONSHIP TO YOU:

COMMENTS/FEEDBACK:

NAME:

CONTACT DETAILS:

RELATIONSHIP TO YOU:

COMMENTS/FEEDBACK:

NAME:

CONTACT DETAILS:

RELATIONSHIP TO YOU:

COMMENTS/FEEDBACK:

Don't let
your ego
hold you
back.
Maybe you'll
fail - but
maybe
you'll fly.

IS THERE ANYTHING LIKE YOUR IDEA ALREADY OUT THERE?

COMPANY #1
COMPANY NAME:
PRODUCT:
WHERE DO THEY SELL IT?
HOW PROFITABLE ARE THEY?

WHAT ARE THEY DOING WELL?

HOW COULD THEY DO IT BETTER?

WHERE IS THE GAP?

COMPANY #2
COMPANY NAME:
PRODUCT:
WHERE DO THEY SELL IT?
HOW PROFITABLE ARE THEY?

WHAT ARE THEY DOING WELL?

HOW COULD THEY DO IT BETTER?

WHERE IS THE GAP?

COMPANY #3
COMPANY NAME:
PRODUCT:
WHERE DO THEY SELL IT?
HOW PROFITABLE ARE THEY?

WHAT ARE THEY DOING WELL?

HOW COULD THEY DO IT BETTER?

WHERE IS THE GAP?

(The best way to predict your future is to create it.)
—Abraham Lincoln

CULTURE UP

IN AN IDEAL WORLD, WHEN WOULD YOU LIKE TO WORK? (TICK AS MANY BOXES AS APPLY)

☐ I START EARLY AND FINISH EARLY

☐ I START LATE AND FINISH LATE

☐ I NEVER WORK WEEKENDS

☐ I LIKE STRUCTURE AND ROUTINE

☐ NO TWO DAYS ARE THE SAME

☐ I WORK SIX MONTHS ON AND SIX MONTHS OFF

☐ I WORK AS LITTLE AS POSSIBLE

☐ OTHER:

IN AN IDEAL WORLD, WHERE WOULD YOU LIKE TO WORK? (TICK AS MANY BOXES AS APPLY)

- ☐ IN AN OFFICE ENVIRONMENT

- ☐ FROM HOME

- ☐ WITH MY LAPTOP IN A CAFÉ

- ☐ IN A PARK

- ☐ AT THE BEACH

- ☐ AT A CO-WORKING SPACE

- ☐ TRAVELLING AROUND THE COUNTRY

- ☐ TRAVELLING AROUND THE WORLD

- ☐ ALWAYS ON THE MOVE

- ☐ ALWAYS FROM THE SAME PLACE

- ☐ OTHER:

IN AN IDEAL WORLD, WHAT WOULD YOU LIKE TO WEAR AT WORK?

- [ ] SUIT

- [ ] CORPORATE GET-UP

- [ ] WORKOUT WEAR

- [ ] THE LATEST FASHION

- [ ] JEANS AND A T-SHIRT

- [ ] WHATEVER I WEAR AT THE WEEKEND

- [ ] THE CLOSEST OUTFIT IN MY WARDROBE

- [ ] MY PYJAMAS

- [ ] OTHER:

WHERE DO YOU FEEL MOST INSPIRED?

WHERE DO YOU FEEL MOST CREATIVE?

WHERE DO YOU FEEL MOST PRODUCTIVE?

X

X

X

X

WHERE ARE YOU MOST LIKELY TO BE DISTRACTED?

X

X

X

X

(It's your road and yours alone. — Rumi)

COMPANY CULTURES I LOVE AND WHY:

COMPANY #1:

WHAT I LOVE ABOUT THEIR CULTURE:

WHAT I CAN LEARN FROM THEM:

Want to know how I created the collective culture? See P 110. of Daring + Disruptive

COMPANY #2:

WHAT I LOVE ABOUT THEIR CULTURE:

WHAT I CAN LEARN FROM THEM:

COMPANY #3:

WHAT I LOVE ABOUT THEIR CULTURE:

WHAT I CAN LEARN FROM THEM:

COMPANY CULTURES TO AVOID AND WHY:

Make a note to your current and future self, listing workplace cultures you don't want to be a part of or see unfold under your watch:

CULTURAL NO-NO #1:

CULTURAL NO-NO #2:

CULTURAL NO-NO #3:

CULTURAL NO-NO #4:

CULTURAL NO-NO #5

CULTURAL NO-NO #6

my moodboard...

Use these pages to visualise your fantasy work hub – draw, doodle, stick in pages from magazines, sketch pictures, take photos of inspiring places you visit that get your creative juices flowing.

my moodboard...

+ Add to me!

my moodboard...

+ Add to me!

Punch the air, dance around, laugh aloud, inject joy!

INVEST...
IN YOU

Contract of self ♡

I, _____, promise to nurture, invest and protect my best asset – me! No matter how busy, stressed and in demand I get, I vow to always take the time to touch base with myself, to do simple things that make me laugh and to do activities that make me glow.

I promise not to neglect my friends, my family and the people who keep my feet grounded, even when my inbox is close to imploding and my to-do list seems never-ending. I will stop, I will reboot, I will do something – anything – that nourishes my soul.

Signature:

Date:

HOW DO YOU INVEST IN YOUR BODY?

HOW DO YOU INVEST IN YOUR MIND?

HOW DO YOU INVEST IN YOUR SOUL?

FIVE SIMPLE THINGS THAT GROUND ME:

#1

#2

#3

#4

#5

FIVE SONGS THAT INSPIRE ME:

#1

#2

#3

#4

#5

FIVE QUOTES THAT NOURISH ME:

#1

#2

#3

#4

#5

Be your
own guru.
Happiness,
it takes
hard work.

FIND YOUR OWN THERAPY

WHERE IS THE MOST HEALING PLACE YOU'VE EVER VISITED?

WHEN AND WHERE DO YOU FEEL MOST PEACEFUL?

WHERE IS YOUR FAVOURITE PLACE TO MEET FRIENDS
OR FAMILY?

WHAT RITUALS HELP YOU TO RELAX OR UNWIND?

It took me 10 years of personal
development to get to where I
am (really!).
In Daring & Disruptive (page 60)
I share my journey.

Look deep
into nature,
you will
understand
everything
better.

-Albert
Einstein

WHEN WAS THE LAST TIME YOU...

WENT FOR A WALK WITHOUT YOUR MOBILE PHONE:

DELIBERATELY GOT LOST IN YOUR CAR:

PLANNED A SOLO TRIP:

LAID ON A BLANKET IN THE PARK AND WATCHED THE CLOUDS FLOAT BY:

SAT AT A CAFÉ AND LISTENED TO SOMEONE
ELSE'S CONVERSATION:

STROLLED AROUND A MARKET:

WENT SWIMMING IN THE RAIN:

LAUGHED ALONE:

What can you do
(right now) to give
yourself a
five-minute
joy break?

I am allergic to negative people.

Everyone in your inner circle is special for their own reasons. Seek out the people you need for every eventuality.

WHO'S IN YOUR MIX?

WHEN I NEED TO BOUNCE AROUND BIG IDEAS, I CALL:

WHEN I NEED TEA AND SYMPATHY, I CALL:

WHEN I NEED TOUGH LOVE, I CALL:

WHEN I WANT TO DELVE DEEP, I CALL:

WHEN I JUST NEED TO LAUGH, I CALL:

WHEN I NEED TO SIT IN SILENCE WITH SOMEONE, I CALL:

WHAT QUALITIES DO YOU SEEK IN A LIFE PARTNER?

WHAT QUALITIES DO YOU SEEK IN A BUSINESS PARTNER?

MAKE PLANS AND THEN... DO THEM!

There are so many incredible people already in our lives who can teach and inspire us. Ask yourself, who inspires you (friends, family, colleagues, mentors, peers) and why, what you'd love to do with them (have a coffee, walk their dog, pick their brains, collaborate, have them endorse your idea, co-author a book with them, work for them or... be their boss etc). Whatever it may be, think BIG and plan how you can make it happen.

INSPIRED BY #1
NAME:
WHY THEY INSPIRE YOU:

WHAT YOU'LL DO TOGETHER:

SET A DATE/PLAN:

INSPIRED BY #2
NAME:
WHY THEY INSPIRE YOU:

WHAT YOU'LL DO TOGETHER:

SET A DATE/PLAN:

INSPIRED BY #3
NAME:
WHY THEY INSPIRE YOU:

WHAT YOU'LL DO TOGETHER:

SET A DATE/PLAN:

INSPIRED BY #4
NAME:
WHY THEY INSPIRE YOU:

WHAT YOU'LL DO TOGETHER:

SET A DATE/PLAN:

INSPIRED BY #5
NAME:
WHY THEY INSPIRE YOU:

WHAT YOU'LL DO TOGETHER:

SET A DATE/PLAN:

INSPIRED BY #6
NAME:
WHY THEY INSPIRE YOU:

WHAT YOU'LL DO TOGETHER:

SET A DATE/PLAN:

INSPIRED BY #7
NAME:
WHY THEY INSPIRE YOU:

WHAT YOU'LL DO TOGETHER:

SET A DATE/PLAN:

INSPIRED BY #8
NAME:
WHY THEY INSPIRE YOU:

WHAT YOU'LL DO TOGETHER:

SET A DATE/PLAN:

SET YOURSELF SOME PROFESSIONAL INVESTMENT GOALS

CONFERENCES, COURSES OR EVENTS I WANT TO ATTEND THIS YEAR:

HOW I CAN MAKE IT HAPPEN:

✗ Financially

✗ Logistically

BOOKS I WANT TO READ, EVEN WHEN LOVELY MAGAZINES
LIKE *THE COLLECTIVE* (SEE WHAT I DID THERE?)
LURE ME AWAY:

BLOGS I WANT TO FOLLOW:

PROFESSIONAL COFFEES OR LUNCH DATES I'D LOVE TO HAVE:

HOW I CAN MAKE THEM HAPPEN:

(remember people's time is precious
so ensure you offer value exchange.)

THE AMOUNT OF MONEY I VOW TO SPEND ON MYSELF TO INVEST IN MY PROFESSIONAL LIFE:

AND WHAT I'LL SPEND IT ON:

Ignorance is not bliss.

What am I doing to create a happier, safer, better world?

DO GOOD

THERE'S NO 'I' IN WHY

From my first day in business, I made a resolution to help others (although I wasn't sure quite how at that point). That's one of the reasons I overcame my fear of public speaking – I realised that I couldn't connect people and inspire them by being a shivering mouse hiding in a shoebox. I needed a profile and a launch pad. My 'why' needed to be bigger than me.

WHAT DO YOU WANT YOUR LEGACY TO BE?

IMAGINE YOU'RE WRITING YOUR OWN EULOGY (OKAY, IT'S DEPRESSING, BUT A USEFUL TOOL). HOW WOULD YOU LIKE YOUR LIFE'S WORK TO BE DESCRIBED?

TAKING IT A STEP FURTHER (AND THIS WAS A VERY POWERFUL MOMENT FOR ME), WHAT WOULD YOU WANT YOUR TOMBSTONE TO READ?

WHICH CHARITIES OR CAUSES ARE IMPORTANT TO YOU?

IF YOU HAD LIMITLESS MONEY, WHO WOULD YOU HELP?

IF YOU WERE TO VOLUNTEER FOR A CHARITY IN ANY
CAPACITY (EVEN ONE DAY A YEAR), WHO WOULD IT BE FOR
AND WHY?

ANALYSE YOUR EMOTIONS

There is this myth around successful people that we are all stony, heartless robots. But achievement and compassion are not mutually exclusive. I sob at movies, I blub at documentaries, I weep when I hit a milestone that's important to me (and I wrote about it in *Daring and Disruptive* on page 176). I don't fight my emotions – I analyse them! My tears are a barometer for the things that really matter to me and the issues I want to fight for and ultimately see changed.

MOMENT #1
WHAT MOVED ME OR MADE ME CRY?

REASON:

HOW CAN I HELP OR CHANGE THE SITUATION?

MOMENT #2
WHAT MOVED ME OR MADE ME CRY?

REASON:

HOW CAN I HELP OR CHANGE THE SITUATION?

MOMENT #3
WHAT MOVED ME OR MADE ME CRY?

REASON:

HOW CAN I HELP OR CHANGE THE SITUATION?

MOMENT #4
WHAT MOVED ME OR MADE ME CRY?

REASON:

HOW CAN I HELP OR CHANGE THE SITUATION?

MOMENT #5
WHAT MOVED ME OR MADE ME CRY?

REASON:

HOW CAN I HELP OR CHANGE THE SITUATION?

You may say I'm a dreamer, but I'm not the only one

-John Lennon

NOW GO...

HOW WOULD YOU SUM UP YOUR IDEA TO AN INVESTOR?

HOW WOULD YOU DESCRIBE IT TO A RETAILER?

HOW WOULD YOU DESCRIBE IT TO A CUSTOMER FROM
YOUR COUNTRY?

HOW WOULD YOU DESCRIBE IT TO A CUSTOMER WHO
LIVES ABROAD?

BUILDING A BRAND

WHAT DOMAIN NAMES DO YOU NEED TO REGISTER?

WHAT SOCIAL MEDIA HANDLES SHOULD YOU SNAP UP?

WHAT PERSONAL CHARACTERISTICS AND SKILLS MAKE YOU
UNIQUE AND MEMORABLE?

HOW CAN YOU TELL THE WORLD ABOUT THEM?

WRITE YOUR FANTASY BIO:

This year, _____
achieved her/his dream of
_____
_____
_____.
She/he made waves in
the _____ industry
by _____
_____
_____

and is highly regarded
as an expert in _____
_____

In her/his spare time,
_____ is passionate
about _____
_____
_____
_____

and has achieved
a lifelong ambition of
_____
_____
_____
_____ .

WRITE THE SPEECH YOU'LL GIVE AT THE LAUNCH PARTY OF YOUR NEW IDEA

How will you describe your journey? Who will you thank?
What are you most proud of?

I know, I know, your idea is just a twinkle in your eye right now, but one day (hopefully sooner rather than later) you'll be standing at the front of a roomful of interested parties, celebrating the birth of your (business) baby. And believe me, there's no better feeling.

my speech...

Think big from the outset, because that's when the foundations of your dreams are laid.

Imagine
your future
- then
<u>supersize</u> it.

THE BIG PICTURE

I hope the prompts in this book have churned up a wealth of ideas and helped you to focus on your values, hook into your purpose and think about your future. Now, let's bring it all together!

I challenge you to go to your nearest park, find a quiet spot, set an alarm on your phone for 15 minutes, and then pick up a pen and word vomit (one of my favourite phrases) onto the next page until the alarm sounds. By that, I mean… write freely, without hesitation, without overthinking.

I want you to imagine your perfect workday. Not just a good day – an absolutely perfect one. If anything – absolutely anything – was possible and there were no practical or financial constraints, then what would your career look like?

Start with the moment you wake up in the morning – what time is it? Do you go straight to the office? Where do you go to work, who do you work with, what do you wear and what do you do when you get there? How do you feel, what do you achieve, what time do you finish and what is your last thought before you go to sleep?

Maybe you never set foot in an office at all and your average workday involves five minutes of email checking and 23 hours and 55 minutes of beach dwelling. If so, how have you made this happen?

See it, believe it and you're one step closer to living it.

my notes...

stylemaker Scrapbook

The next pages are all yours! Stick in newspaper clippings, printouts, inspirational quotes, ideas, your scribble on the back of napkins, photos of your role models... It will help you stay motivated – and one day be a memento of your journey.

my scrapbook ...

You did it!

Now go,
the
world
is
yours.

ABOUT THE AUTHOR

Lisa Messenger is the vibrant, game-changing CEO and creative director of The Messenger Group, as well as founder and editor-in-chief of *The Collective* magazine – an entrepreneurial and lifestyle magazine distributed into more than 37 countries with a mandate to disrupt, challenge and inspire.

In addition, she has worked globally in events, sponsorship, marketing, PR and publishing, has authored and co-authored over a dozen of her own books while The Messenger Group has custom published more than 400 books for others.

Lisa is a regular commentator on business, entrepreneurialism and property and has sat on a number of boards including the Australian Businesswomen's Network and Publishers Australia. She's trekked across India raising money for charity, ridden camels in the Sahara for fun and has laughed her way through communal showers in the Costa Rican jungle in the name of personal development.

Her passion is to challenge individuals and corporations to change the way they think, to get out of their comfort zones and prove that there is more than one way to do anything. She encourages entrepreneurial spirit, creativity and innovation. In between being a serial entrepreneur and avid traveller, she spends most of her time in Sydney with her partner Jack and their beautiful dog, Benny.

RENEGADE COLLECTIVE

The Collective is a monthly 176-page entrepreneurial and lifestyle magazine that brings together entrepreneurial and creative minds from across the globe and is distributed in more than 37 countries. It's a community that appeals to game changers, rule breakers, thought leaders and style makers with a common appetite for challenging the status quo.

Through personal stories, in-depth interviews, investigative features and practical tips, *The Collective* aims to inspire and inform. Whether you are looking for a new idea to tackle, business advice from industry professionals or a friendly dose of encouragement, *The Collective* is your guide to making an impact in this world.

COLLECTIVE HUB

More than just a print magazine, the Collective Hub global community is engaged across a number of platforms that echo the same philosophies found within our pages. We are reaching out to our readers wherever they are in the world through events, collaborations, strategic partnerships, our ambassador program and ultimately continuing the conversation through our online hubs.

WEBSITE *collectivehub.com*
FACEBOOK *facebook.com/collectivehub*
INSTAGRAM *@lisamessenger #daringanddisruptive*
@collectivehub #collectivehub
TWITTER *@lisamessenger #daringanddisruptive*
@collectivehub #collectivehub

Haven't read the prequel yet?

DARING & DISRUPTIVE: UNLEASHING THE ENTREPRENEUR

Daring & Disruptive is an insightful and soulful account of the entrepreneur's roller-coaster ride for those who want to succeed almost as much as they want to breathe… who want to make the impossible possible and the ordinary extraordinary.

Lisa gives readers a valuable insight into her world, whether you're a budding entrepreneur, seasoned game changer or a corporate ladder-climber dreaming of creating your own gig or making positive change from the inside. This book will help you dig deep, stay on purpose, back yourself, be true to your ideas, and ensure that if you're thrown to the wolves, you'll have the strength to come out leading the pack.

As *New York Times'* best-selling author Bradley Trevor Grieve, AM, says: *"Business anarchy for fun and profit – not for the short of breath, weak of spine or faint of heart. Put on clean underwear and turn to page one."*